Walter Bachinski

Walter Bachinski, 2000

Walter Bachinski

2000

GdB GALERIE DE BELLEFEUILLE

1367, avenue Greene, Montréal, Québec H3Z 2A8 téléphone : (514) 933-4406 télécopieur : (514) 933-6553 www.debellefeuille.com

Gertrude Stein reçut un jour, d'un magazine qui l'avait publiée, un questionnaire où on lui demandait ce qu'elle pensait de l'art moderne. Elle répondit : « J'aime le regarder ». On oublie facilement ce que l'on est censé faire devant un tableau : le regarder. On n'a pas à le « traquer » systématiquement, comme semblent si souvent le faire les critiques, qui se bardent de faits et s'acharnent à être subtils, mais trahissent l'indigence de leur faculté d'étonnement, persuadés qu'une formule narquoise restera longtemps gravée à l'esprit. On est censé le regarder — se tenir devant lui et se servir de nos yeux. On devrait le remarquer, et non faire des remarques. On devrait se souvenir. Apprendre et s'étonner.

Devant les tableaux de Walter Bachinski, on a la bonne fortune d'être stupéfait. Des choses de tous les jours — des fleurs, une chaise, un visage, des fenêtres — revêtent des formes nouvelles. Ce que l'on voit sur la toile n'est pas ce que l'on verrait si l'on était placé devant ces fleurs ou cette fenêtre ouvrant sur un jardin, mais on est en quelque sorte en pays de connaissance. On connaît ces choses, sous les apparences, sur le pourtour de l'œil. La faculté de rendre familiers les objets essentiels est une des nombreuses qualités de l'artiste, et la stupéfaction du spectateur constitue l'aveu de sa dette. En état de stupéfaction, il peut commencer à apprendre.

En art, le meilleur donne toujours le même choc. Dans *A Summer Garden*, Emily Dickinson dit : « Tels des wagons de train sur des rails en peluche / J'entends le bourdonnement régulier de l'abeille », et il est là, dans nos oreilles, le bruit de l'abeille dans l'air chaud qui étouffe les sons. D'un seul trait, Matisse crée non seulement un dos, mais aussi les muscles et la tension qui le soutiennent, et on peut passer la main sur ce dos. Dans la mélodie de *Im Frühling*, de Schubert, on entend une journée de printemps, mais la joie que procure cette mélodie est nôtre. Il ne s'agit pas du fait — quoi qu'en disent les théoriciens actuels de la déconstruction — que l'on arrive devant un poème, un tableau ou un air avec notre expérience, et que l'on en devient co-créateur. Bien entendu, on arrive avec son moi, de la même manière que l'on arrive avec sa bonne volonté à une réunion d'amis. On arrive avec sa faculté de récognition et, quand le poète, le compositeur ou le peintre nous montre une vérité, on apprend. Ce que l'on expérimente n'est pas la création, mais la re-création.

Devant ces tableaux, on évoque ce que l'on a vu, les peintures que l'on a vues, parce que, comme tant d'autres artistes accomplis, Walter Bachinski nourrit son travail des traditions et des œuvres de ses prédécesseurs. À une époque aguichée par l'« originalité », on oublie que l'originalité n'est pas affaire de nouveauté mais d'origines, et que de siècle en siècle, les grands artistes ne se ressemblent que dans la mesure où ils ont traité les mêmes thèmes. Après tout, l'histoire des œuvres humaines en est une d'alluvionnement. Héraclite l'a énoncé clairement : « On ne se baigne jamais deux fois dans le même fleuve », Et Spenser, rendant hommage à Chaucer dans *The Faerie Queene*, écrit :

> par la douce infusion
> De ton propre esprit, qui en moi te survit,
> J'attache ici mon pas à tes pas.

Walter Bachinski ouvre les yeux du spectateur comme doit le faire un artiste. Ses tableaux sont beaux, pas seulement décoratifs. Ainsi, quand on regarde *Bouquet of Spring Flowers*

[page 37], on entre dans un lieu complexe et immémorial. Même si on ne pratique pas l'art du dessin, on prend conscience, comme dans le souvenir d'autres tableaux, du langage technique de la ligne, tandis que l'on suit la courbe du bord de la table, et son écho dans celle de l'étang à l'arrière-plan; on sent, à sa gauche, le raidissement du trait vertical de l'encadrement de la porte et la tension créée par les courbes qui animent l'espace qu'elles délimitent, dans lequel s'épanouit le rose d'un arbre en fleur; on crée un syntagme de ce rose contre le nuage violet qui le domine et l'étang bleu à ses pieds, et de la manière dont le rose s'étire pour rejoindre, telle une corde, le rouge de la table; et on perçoit les harmonies de basse de la verticale bleu sombre, à gauche, et du rougeoiement profond de la verticale à droite, comme si leur rôle était de rappeler le ton du tableau, de fournir une rime qui mette fin à la contemplation. On apprend ces choses en regardant, on trouve des analogies dans des souvenirs familiers, mais on se remémore aussi : devant chaque tableau réussi, on recrée les formes à la fois physiques et culturelles du monde.

Ainsi, les formes de l'art nous rappellent notre place dans un plan qui nous dépasse. En d'autres termes, on peut aussi bien découvrir qui on est en contemplant ce tableau qu'en lisant les philosophes. « Mais ce ne sont pas des fleurs », pourrait-on dire. « C'est un tableau qui représente des fleurs ». C'est exact. Le tableau montre l'essence des fleurs — la « floralité » — et il évoque aussi une tradition que les Français ont appelée l'« intimisme », selon laquelle il était parfaitement raisonnable de considérer les éléments de la vie quotidienne de l'artiste — les gens, les animaux et les objets qui l'entourent — comme aussi valables que d'autres pour commencer à explorer la vie. L'idée n'était pas nouvelle; comme le disaient les Florentins : *Ogni dipintore dipinge se* (Tout peintre est son propre sujet). La réussite d'un tableau comme *Bouquet of Spring Flowers* réside dans le fait qu'il transcende la banalité et nous révèle que les choses ordinaires de la vie comportent un début de sagesse — qu'il suffit de regarder.

Ce regard peut être ardu, et saisissant. Les tableaux de Walter Bachinski sont séduisants et profondément ravissants. Les fleurs, la beauté froide des figures classiques, la pure magie des gens du cirque, la sérénité des pièces remplies de lumière et de couleur, tout inspire au spectateur une vive admiration pour le talent de l'artiste, et une joie reconnaissante pour le plaisir qu'il offre aux sens. Les tableaux sont charmants — et vrais. Je songe au profil d'Orphée dans *Orpheus with Classical Bust* [page 19], dont la ligne meurtrie, douce, tendue s'est gravée dans mon esprit dès que je l'ai vu, il y a des semaines. Je l'ai gardé en mémoire, l'y ai revu maintes fois, et j'ai senti son ombre un peu mélancolique en lisant ou en me promenant. J'y vois l'avatar du dessin, l'essence d'une tradition, quelque chose de presque détaché de ce monde. Et un jour où je marchais dans une rue de Vancouver, derrière un jeune homme en guenilles, une épave ballottée, quand je l'ai vu se tourner pour regarder une vitrine, j'ai eu l'impression que les éléments me faisaient signe, car c'était son profil qui était dans le tableau, émergeant des haillons, de la pluie et du bruit habituel de la rue. Voilà ce que je veux dire quand je dis qu'une image est vraie, quand je dis que regarder les tableaux de Walter Bachinski apporte la bénédiction et la bonne fortune d'être stupéfait.

Crispin Elsted, 2000
traduit par Christine Gendreau

Crispin Elsted est poète, typographe et copropriétaire de Barbarian Press. *Son récent livre de poésie* Climate and Affections *a été mis en nomination pour le prix littéraire du Gouverneur Général du Canada.*

Gertrude Stein once was sent a questionnaire from a magazine which had published her work, and in it she was asked what she felt about modern art. She said, "I like to look at it." It is easy to forget that looking at a picture is what we are supposed to do with it. We are not obliged to stalk it, as critics so often seem to, bristling with facts, hellbent on cleverness and short on wonder, determined that some pawky phrase will be remembered long after the picture has been seen.

We are supposed to look at it – to stand in front of it and to use our eyes. We should take note, but not take notes. We should remember. We should learn, and wonder.

Looking at Walter Bachinski's pictures, we have the good fortune to be amazed. Everyday things – flowers, a chair, a face, windows – become combed with fresh assumptions. What we see in the image is not what we would see ourselves if we were to look at such flowers or encounter such a window opening out on a garden, but we recognise it somehow. We know it, somewhere under the sight, at the side of the eye. To make the essentials familiar is one of his many gifts, and our amazement is the statement of our debt. In that amazement we can begin to learn.

The best in art always gives us the same shock: Emily Dickinson, in "A Summer Garden", says: "Like trains of cars on tracks of plush / I hear the level bee" and it is there in our ears, the sound of the bee in hot, muffled air. Matisse, in a single line, creates not just a back, but the muscles and tension supporting it, and we can stroke that back beneath our hand. The melody of Schubert's "Im Frühling" is the sound a Spring day makes, but the joy in that melody is ours. It is not – whatever the current theorists of deconstruction may say – that we bring our own experience to a poem, or a picture, or a tune, and become its co-creators. Of course we bring our selves, just as we bring our good will to a gathering of friends. We bring the capacity for recognition, and when the poet or composer or painter shows us a truth, we learn. What we experience is not creation, but recreation.

Looking at these pictures, we remember what we have seen, and what we have seen painted, because like so many fine artists, Walter Bachinski draws on the traditions and works of his predecessors to inform his work. In an age randy for "originality", we forget that originality deals not with novelty, but with origins, and that the great artists of any age are alike only in that they share the same themes. The history of anything human is a history of accretion, after all. Herakleitos made the point: "You can never step twice into the same river." And Spenser, paying tribute to Chaucer in *The Faerie Queene*, says

> through infusion sweet
> Of thine own spirit, which doth in me survive,
> I follow here the footing of thy feet.

Walter Bachinski opens our eyes as an artist should. His pictures are beautiful, but they are not merely decorative. So, for example, when we look at the picture called "Bouquet of Spring Flowers" [Plate 37] we enter a complex and immemorial place. Even if we do

not draw, we become aware, as in a memory of other pictures we have looked at, of the technical language of line as we follow the curve of the table's edge, and its echo in the curve of the distant pond behind it; we feel the stiffening of the vertical line of the doorway to its left, and the tension between that and the curves which enlivens the space they bracket, in which a tree blossoms a yielding pink; we make a syntax of the pink against the violet cloud above it and the blue pond below, and the way the pink reaches over to connect like a chord with the red of the table; and we see the bass harmonies of the deep blue vertical on the left and the deep red glow of the vertical on the right of the picture, as if they were to remind us of the key of the picture, to provide a rhyme to close the process of looking. We learn these things as we look, finding analogies in familiar memories, but we also remember: we recreate with every good picture the forms of the world, both physical and cultural.

So the forms of art remind us of our place in a scheme outside ourselves. It is, in other words, as possible to discover our selves in contemplating this picture as in reading philosophers. "But these are not flowers", we may think. "This is a picture of flowers." It is. It shows us the essence of flowers – "flowerness" – and it also recalls a tradition which the French called "Intimism", in which it was considered perfectly reasonable that the day-to-day elements of the artist's life, the people and animals and things which surrounded him, were as good a place to begin the exploration of life as any other. The idea was not new: as the Florentines said, *Ogni dipintore dipinge se.* ('Every painter is his own subject.') The success of a picture like "Bouquet of Spring Flowers" is in its transcendence of the commonplace, and its revelation that the common things in our own lives have the beginnings of wisdom in them – if only we will look.

That looking can be arduous, and startling. Walter Bachinski's pictures are beguiling and profoundly lovely. The flowers, the cool beauty of the classical figures, the real magic of the circus people, the serene rooms full of light and colour, all bring us to a feeling admiration for his gifts as an artist, and a grateful joy for the pleasure he gives our senses. The pictures are lovely – and true. I think of the bruised, sweet, taut line of the profile of Orpheus in "Orpheus With Classical Bust" [page 19] , which has settled in my mind's eye since I first saw it, weeks ago. I have held it in memory, looked at it again and again, and felt its slightly melancholy shadow as I read, or walked. It seems to me the avatar of drawing, the essence of a tradition, something almost otherworldly. And walking down a street in Vancouver behind a derelict, a ragged, tossed young man, I saw him turn to look into a storefront window, and felt as if nudged by weather, because it was his profile that was in the picture, surging from the rags and the rain and the common noise of the street. That is what I mean when I say an image is true. And that is what I mean when I say that, looking at Walter Bachinski's pictures, we have the blessed good fortune to be amazed.

Crispin Elsted, 2000

Crispin Elsted is a poet, typographer, and co-proprietor of Barbarian Press. His recent book of poetry Climate and Affections *was listed for the Governor General's Literary Award.*

The Sculptor's Studio
Pastel
59 ½″ x 80 ¼″

Blue Room, Red Table, Red Shutters
Pastel
28 ¾" x 40 ⅝"

14

The Still Life Painter
Pastel
37³/₄″ x 57¹/₄″

Blue Room, White Shutters
Pastel
41" x 29"

Amaryllis in Pale Blue Vase
pastel
38 1/2" x 25 3/8"

Orpheus with Classical Bust
Pastel
59 5/8" x 39 3/4"

Circus Life, the Procession
Pastel
59 1/2" x 35"

The Music of Spring
Pastel
38″ x 59½″

Circus Performer
Pastel
15 5/8" X 11"

Circus Life, the Magician
Pastel
39 ¾″ x 59 ¾″

Studio Still Life II
Pastel
46 3/8" x 33 3/8"

Cyclamen and Fruit on Wrought Iron Chair
Pastel
45″ x 20¼″

The Still Life Painter with Red Table
Pastel
29" x 28⅛"

Studio Still Life I
Pastel
50 ³/₈″ x 35 ¹/₂″

Anemones and Fruit on Wrought Iron Chair
Pastel
29" x 26¾"

Circus Life,
the Performance
Pastel
39 3/8" x 59 3/4"

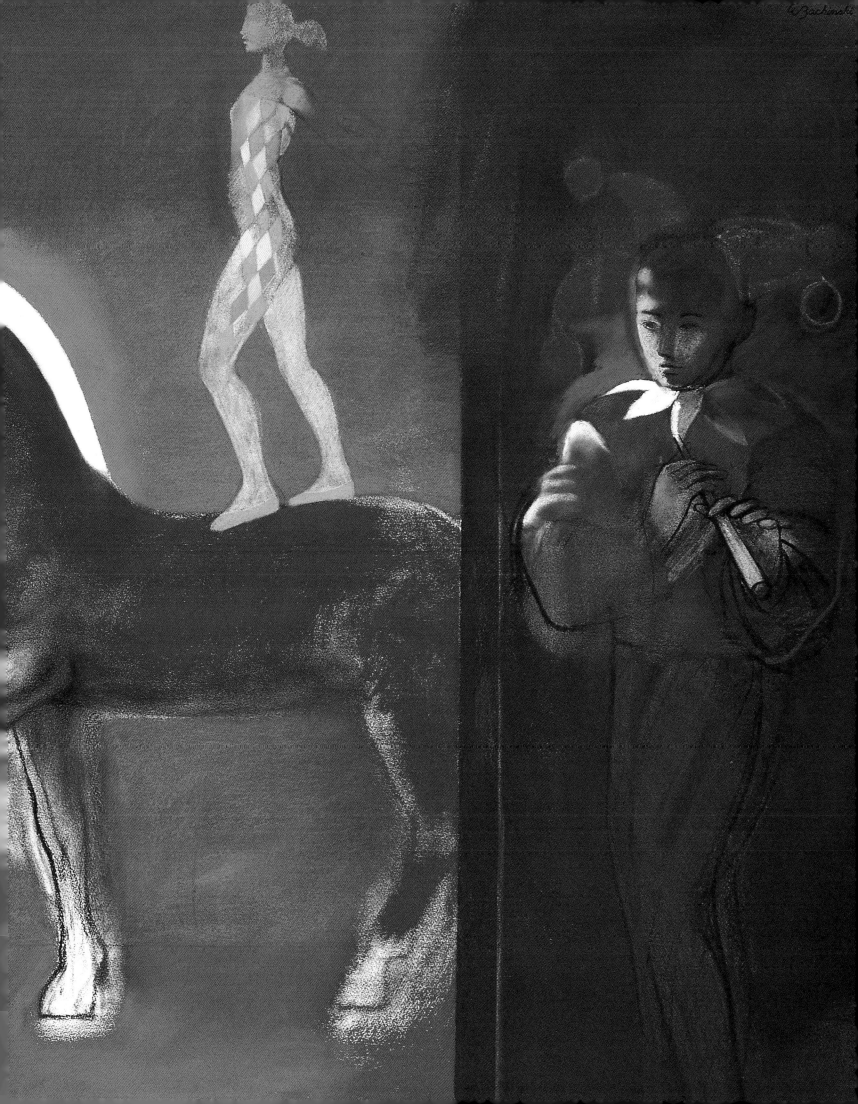

Music
Pastel
44 ¼" x 20"

Souvenirs of Cagnes-sur-Mer, Venus Victorious
Pastel
52 1/4" x 27 1/2"

Anemones in White Pot
Pastel
29 1/4″ x 38 1/2″

Anemones, Spring Breezes
Pastel
29 ½″ x 29″

Bouquet of Spring Flowers
Pastel
44 1/8" x 27 1/2"

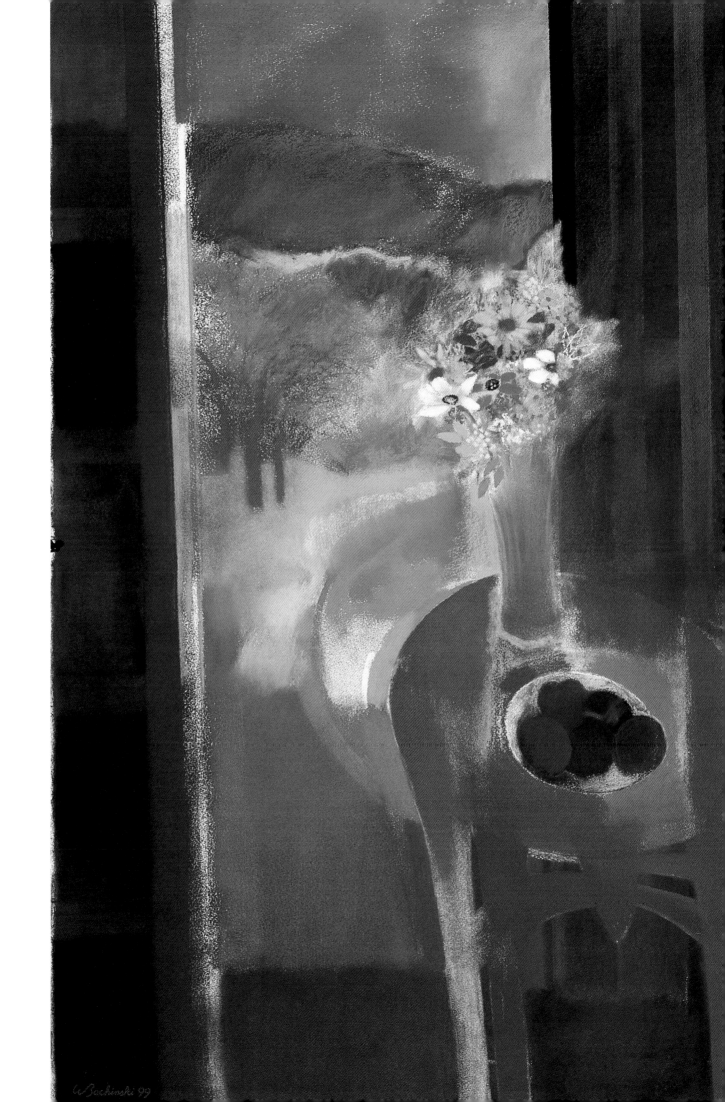

Head of a Dancer
Pastel
17 1/4″ x 13 1/2″

Night Flower
Pastel
24 5/8″ x 17 1/2

The Gray Horse
Pastel
39 ³/₄″ x 59 ⁵/₈″

Janis with Hands Grasped
Pastel
22" x 18 ¼"

Né à Ottawa en 1939, Walter Bachinski a étudié au Ontario College of Art, travaillant en étroite collaboration avec Frederick Hagan. Il est diplômé de l'institution en 1965. Il complétera, deux ans plus tard, une maîtrise à l'université d'Iowa, sous la direction de Mauricio Lasansky. Walter Bachinski a aussitôt entamé une carrière d'enseignement à l'université de Guelph où il accède au rang de professeur titulaire en 1984. Toutefois, il devra réduire son engagement professoral afin de se consacrer plus activement à sa carrière artistique. Il met un terme à sa carrière universitaire en 1994.

Walter Bachinski a beaucoup voyagé, étudiant au Mexique les oeuvres murales d'Orozco et de Siquerios, et s'installant temporairement en France (1978-1979) afin de mieux étudier les chefs-d'oeuvre (particulièrement français) de la fin du XIXe et des débuts du XXe siècle. Il poursuivra ses recherches sur ces périodes artistiques à travers de nombreuses collections, tant en France qu'aux État-unis.

Ses premières oeuvres se présentaient principalement en noir et blanc, alors que l'artiste se consacrait surtout à la gravure et au dessin. Par la suite, il a commencé à s'intéresser à la sculpture en ronde-bosse et en bas-relief. Régulièrement, ses oeuvres feront référence à la mythologie. En 1975, il introduit le thème de la mère et l'enfant, puis, celui de l'artiste et son modèle. C'est lors d'un séjour en France (1978-1979) que Bachinski porte son regard sur la nature morte et qu'il commence à utiliser le pastel afin de développer un art exploitant habilement les richesses de la couleur. Depuis 1994, Bachinski vit et travaille à Shanty Bay, en Ontario.

Walter Bachinski was born in 1939 in Ottawa. He worked closely with Frederick Hagan at the Ontario College of Art, graduating in 1965, and went on to complete his Master's Degree at the University of Iowa under the direction of Mauricio Lasansky in 1967. Shortly thereafter he began teaching at the University of Guelph, gaining tenure in 1970 and progressing through the ranks to Full Professor in 1984. At that time he began reducing his teaching, eventually leaving the University in 1994.

Bachinski has travelled extensively throughout his career, at first studying the mural work of Orozco and Siquerios in Mexico and later the museums of Europe to see first hand the great works of the past. Eventually he focused on the masterpieces (particularly French) of the late 19th and early 20th century art

housed in collections in France and the United States.

The very early work was primarily black and white and concentrated on the areas of printmaking and drawing. He began working on sculpture in the round and relief in the early 1970s. In 1975 Bachinski introduced the Mother and Child theme and shortly thereafter the Artist and Model. His work continued to evolve, becoming more classical in style; his exploration of colour in pastels, leading to his re-examination of the possibilities of still life, began in 1978-79 during an extended stay in France. Since 1994, Walter Bachinski has devoted himself exclusively to his art in his studio in Shanty Bay, Ontario.

Expositions individuelles - Selected Solo Exhibitions
* catalogue

2000   *Walter Bachinski 2000**, Galerie de Bellefeuille, Montréal.

1996   *Walter Bachinski, Recent Work**, Galerie de Bellefeuille, Montréal.
       Walter Bachinski: A Fifteen Year Survey of Prints, Erindale College, University of Toronto.

1995   Robertson Galleries, Ottawa.

1993   Galerie de Bellefeuille, Montréal.

1992   *Bachinski: Still Life - Ten Years**, MacLaren Art Centre, Barrie, Ontario.
       Drabinsky Gallery, Toronto.

1991   *Approaching Classicism**, Kitchener-Waterloo Art Gallery, Ontario.
       Heffel Gallery, Vancouver.

1990   Wilfred Laurier University, Waterloo, Ontario.

1989   Robertson Galleries, Ottawa.
       Heffel Gallery, Vancouver.

1987   Gallery Moos, Toronto.

1986   Robertson Galleries, Ottawa.
       Gallery Moos, Toronto.

1985   Macdonald Stewart Art Centre, Guelph, Ontario.

1984   Galerie l'Art Français, Montréal.
       Gallery Moos, Toronto.
       Wilfred Laurier University, Waterloo, Ontario.

1982   Gallery Moos, Toronto.

Expositions de groupe - Selected Group Exhibitions
* catalogue

1999   *Sculptures*, Galerie de Bellefeuille, Montréal.
       The Human Figure in Contemporary Art, Galerie de Bellefeuille, Montréal.
       Art Expo, John Szoke Editions, New York.
       Naked Emotion, Kitchener-Waterloo Art Gallery, Kitchener, Ontario.

1998 *Museologic*, Art Gallery of Mississauga, Ontario.
Three Master Printmakers, Wallace Galleries, Calgary.
New Etchings and Pastels, John Szoke Gallery, New York.
Great Canadian Art for a Great Canadian Cause, Ron Moore Gallery, Toronto.

1997 *Here's Looking at Me Kid: Artists Look at Themselves*, Art Gallery of North York, Ontario.

1995 *Printmakers at Riverside**, Kitchener-Waterloo Art Gallery, Kitchener, Ontario. Exposition itinérante / Travelling exhibition.
One year Later... Additions to the Permanent Collection, Art Gallery of North York, Ontario.

1993 *Practice and Pedagogy*, London Regional Art Museum, London, Ontario.
A Show of CATS: The Feline in Art, Prior Editions, Vancouver.

1992 *The Print Defined*, The Blyth Art Gallery, Blyth, Ontario.
Galerie de Bellefeuille, Montréal.

1990 *Red*, Durham Art Gallery, Ontario.

1989 *Blue*, Durham Art Gallery, Ontario.

1988 *Yellow*, Durham Art Gallery, Ontario.
The Object is the Object, Georgian College, Barrie, Ontario.

1986 *V Bienal americana de artes graficas**, Museo de Arte Moderno, Cali, Colombie.

1985 *Celebrating 20 Years: 1965-1985**, University of Guelph, Faculty of Fine Arts, Macdonald Stewart Art Centre, Guelph, Ontario.

1983-84 *The Hand Holding the Brush: Self-Portraits by Canadian Artists**, London Regional Art Gallery. Tournée nationale / National tour.

1982 *Variations: Bachinski, Chu, Green, Urquhart**, Wellington County Museum, Elora, Ontario.

1981 *Viewpoints: 29 by 9**, Art Gallery of Hamilton, Ontario. Tournée régionale / Regional tour.
Art For Architecture*, The Macdonald Gallery, Toronto.

1980 *Sculpture from Public Collections in Ontario: 1950-1980*, Burlington Cultural Centre, Ontario.

1977 *Visitors, Exiles and Residents: Artists Since 1827**, University of Guelph, Ontario.

1976 *Spectrum Canada**, Royal Canadian Academy. Exposition itinérante / Travelling exhibition.
Portraits on Paper, Morris Gallery, Toronto.
Four Canadian Printmakers*, Central Washington State College, Ellensburg, Wa.
Ontario Now*, Art Gallery of Hamilton, Ontario.
International Sculptures, Gallery Moos, Toronto.
Of Human Bondage*, The Robert McLaughlin Gallery, Oshawa, Ontario. Exposition itinérante / Travelling exhibition.

1974 *5e Biennale internationale de la gravure**, Cracovie, Pologne.
Commonwealth Art Gallery, Londres.
Bachinski, Urquhart, Weinstein, Kitchener-Waterloo Art Gallery, Kitchener, Ontario.

Contemporary Canadian Prints & Drawings, McMaster University Art Gallery, Hamilton, Ontario.
IV International Biennial of Graphic Art, Florence, Italie.
Graphics Canadian, Art Gallery of Ontario. Exposition itinérante / Travelling exhibition.

1973 *Canadian Printmakers*, University of Windsor, Windsor, Ontario.

1972 *Three Canadian Printmakers*, Art Gallery of Brant, Brantford, Ontario.
XI Bienniale of Prints & Drawings*, Lugano, Suisse.

1971 *Exposition internationale des arts graphiques**, Musée des beaux-arts de Montréal, Montréal.

1970 *Canadian Graphics, Canadian Society of Graphic Art*, Toronto.
Adams and Yves Gallery, Toronto.

1969 *Young American Printmakers*, Southern Methodist University, Texas.

1968-69 *Three Printmakers*, Musée des beaux-arts du Canada. Exposition itinérante / Travelling exhibition.

1968 *35th Annual Exhibition*, Canadian Society of Graphic Art, London, Ontario.

1967 *38th Northwest Printmakers International Exhibition*, Seattle.

Bibliographie - Selected Bibliography

Monographies - Books:

1989 Burnett, David, *Cineplex Odeon: The First Ten Years*, Cineplex Odeon Corporation, Toronto.

1984 Bayer, Fern, *The Ontario Collection*, Fitzhenry and Whiteside, Toronto.

1982 Parkin, Jeanne, William Boyle (éd.), *Art in Architecture (Art for the Built Environment in the Province of Ontario)*, Visual Arts of Ontario, Toronto.

1980 Morris, Jerrold, *100 Years of Canadian Drawing*, Methuen, Toronto.

Catalogues:

2000 Elsted, Crispin, *Walter Bachinski, 2000*, Galerie de Bellefeuille, Montréal.

1996 Cumming, Glen, *Walter Bachinski, Recent Work*, Galerie de Bellefeuille, Montréal

1992 Moore, William, *Walter Bachinski: Still Life-Ten Years*, MacLaren Art Centre, Barrie, Ontario.

1991 Cumming, Glen, *Walter Bachinski: Approaching Classicism*, Kitchener-Waterloo Art Gallery, Kitchener, Ontario.

1981 Cumming, Glen, Dr. Thomas Tritschler, Joe Plaskett, *Walter Bachinski: Sculpture and Drawing*, Art Gallery of Hamilton, Hamilton, Ontario.

1976 Ihrig, Robert, Paul Duval, *Bachinski: A Decade*, Kitchener-Waterloo Art Gallery, Kitchener, Ontario.

1972   Weinstein, Alan, *Walter Bachinski*, Nova Scotia
        Art Gallery and Museum, Mount St. Vincent
        University, Halifax, Nouvelle-Écosse.

Catalogues (expositions de groupe - group exhibitions) :

1995   *Printmakers at Riverside*, Kitchener-Waterloo Art
        Gallery, Kitchener, Ontario.
1991   *The Claridge Collection*, publié en l'honneur du 60e
        anniversaire de Charles Bronfman / published in
        honour of the 60th birthday of Charles Bronfman,
        Claridge, Montréal.
1991   *The Peacekeeping Monument Competition*,
        National Capital Commission, Ottawa.
1986   *V bienal americana de artes graficas*, Museo de
        Arte Moderno, Cali, Colombie.
1985   *Celebrating 20 Years, 1965-1985*, University of
        Guelph Fine Art Faculty Exhibition, 22 nov.
        1985-5 jan. 1986, Macdonald Stewart Art
        Centre, Guelph, Ontario.
1983   *The Hand Holding the Brush, Self-portraits by
        Canadian Artists*, une exposition itinérante
        organisée par la London Regional Art Gallery / a
        National Travelling exhibition organized by the
        London Regional Art Gallery, 4 nov. 1983-16
        déc. 1984.
1982   *Variations*, Elora, Ontario, 6 août-6 sept. 1982.
1982   *Graphic Newfoundland*, Burnaby, B.C., avril1982.
1981   *Art for the Architecture, (Selections from the
        Government of Ontario Art Collection). 1966-1981*,
        The Macdonald Gallery, Toronto, 27 mai-4 juil.
        1981.
1981   *Viewpoint, Twenty-nine by Nine*, Art Gallery of
        Hamilton, Hamilton, 8 jan.-22 fév. 1981.
1977   *100 Years, Evolution of the Ontario College of Art*,
        Art Gallery of Ontario, Toronto, 5 nov. 1976-2
        jan. 1977.
1976   *Four Canadian Printmakers*, Central Washington
        State College, Ellensburg, Wa, jan. 1976.
1976   *Of Human Bondage*, The Robert McLaughlin
        Gallery, Oshawa, 28 avril-23 mai 1976.
1976   *Spectrum Canada*, Complexe Desjardins,
        Montréal, 5-31 juillet 1976.
1976   *Ontario Now, A Survey of Contemporary Art*,
        The Art Gallery of Hamilton, Hamilton,
        6-29 fév. 1976.
1974   *Biennale internationale de la gravure*, Cracovie,
        Pologne, 1974.
1972   *L'Internazionale Grafici Lugano 1972*, Museo
        Civico di bell art, Lugano, Suisse,1er août-22
        oct. 1972.
1971   *International Exhibition of Graphics*, Musée des
        beaux-arts de Montréal, Montréal, 23 juin-15
        août 1971.

Revues d'art - Art periodicals

1996   Grande, John, « Un Classique Contemporain »,
        Vie des arts, no 162, printemps, p. 65-67.

1995   Cyr, Mario, « Walter Bachinski, Subtil et
        Complexe », *Parcours*, vol. 1, no 3, p. 80-81.
1993   Yaffe, Phylllis C., « Walter Bachinski à la Galerie
        de Bellefeuille », *Magazin'Art*, no 3, printemps, p.
        45-48, 83-84.
1992   McPherson, Anne, « Walter Bachinski:
        Approaching Classicism », *Extension* (Print and
        Drawing Council of Canada Quarterly), vol.1, no
        3, hiver, p. 8-10.
1991   Cauthery, Ian, « Interview with Walter Bachinski »,
        Carousel Magazine, no 3, p. 16-23.
1984   Lorentzen, Laile, « The Freshness of Tradition »,
        Espace, été, p. 16.
1982   Webb, Marshall H., « Walter Bachinski at Gallery
        Moos », *Artmagazine*, décembre, p. 38-39.
1977   Theobald, Sharon, « Waterloo: Walter Bachinski
        in Retrospective », *Artmagazine*, août-sept., p.14.
1975   Hevig, Judy, « Review », *Artmagazine*, été, p. 7-8.

Journaux - Newspapers:

1996   Bernatchez, Raymond, « Une oeuvre actuelle,
        classique et moderne », *La Presse*, Montréal, 20
        avril, p. D16.
1991   Reid, Robert, « Outside the Mainstream », *The
        Kitchener-Waterloo Record*, Kitchener, 2 oct., p. F1.
1990   Reid, Robert, « Personal Views », *The Kitchener-
        Waterloo Record*, Kitchener, 14 nov., p. 2.
1989   Baele, Nancy, « In the Tradition of Degas », *The
        Ottawa Citizen*, Ottawa, 28 sept., p. F1.
1988   Reid, Robert, « Eloquent Art », *The Kitchener-
        Waterloo Record*, Kitchener, 25 août, p. C1, C3-C4.
1988   Anderson, Rosemary, « Artist Goes to the
        Movies», *The Daily Mercury*, Guelph, 11 août, p. 13.
1985   Kritzwiser, Kay, « A Preoccupation with Women »,
        The Globe & Mail, Toronto, 3 déc., p. C6.
1984   Kritzwiser, Kay, « A Remembrance of Masters Past »,
        The Globe & Mail, Toronto, 27 oct., p. 15.
1981   Kritzwiser, Kay,« Bachinski's Family a Classical
        Treat », *The Globe & Mail*, Toronto, 24 avril, p. 21.
1981   Inglis, Grace, « Female Studies in Great Show at
        Art Gallery », *The Spectator*, Hamilton, 25 avril,
        p. 57.
1980   Hoover, Dorothy, « Portraits », *Alumnus
        Newsletter*, Ontario College of Art, Toronto,
        automne.
1980   Wilson, Trish, « Bronze Nude to Grace the Art
        Gallery Grounds », *The Kitchener-Waterloo
        Record*, Kitchener, 18 sept.
1979   Purdie, James, « Luminous Harmony Sealed in
        Bronze », *The Globe & Mail*, Toronto, 9 sept.,
        p. 14.
1979   Littmann, Sol, « Two Powerful Weekend Shows »,
        The Sunday Star, Toronto, 7 oct., p. B6.
1977   Purdie, James, « Explorations of the Frontiers of
        Time », *The Globe & Mail*, Toronto, 23 avril.
        « Bachinski Hurdles the Bronze Barrier », *The
        Globe & Mail*, Toronto, 10 août, p. 2.
1977   Malone, Judy, « Bachinski in Retrospect », *The

Free Press, London, Ontario, mars.

1976   Purdie, James, « A Big, Bold Survey of Great Sculptures », *The Globe & Mail*, Toronto, 3 avril.

1975   Mackenzie, Susan, « First of Two New Sculptures Is Installed on U.W. Campus », *Kitchener-Waterloo Record*, Kitchener, 16 août.
V. N., « The Violence of Goya, but Echoes of Blake », *The Gazette*, Montréal, mars.

1975   Lehmann, Henry, Georges Bogardi, « Bachinski Forms Sensual, Organic », *Montreal Star*, Montréal, 19 mars.

1974   Sheppard, Jenny, « Despair Dominant in Art Show », *The Spectator*, Hamilton, 16 nov., p. 30.

1971   Kritzwiser, Kay, « Printmakers », *The Globe and Mail*, Toronto, 6 nov. p. 28.

Commandes publiques - Public commissions

1992   Mines and Minerals Research Centre, Laurentian University, Sudbury, Ontario.
1988   Cineplex Odeon Theatre, Kitchener, Ontario.
1985   Donald Forster Sculpture Park, Macdonald Stewart Art Centre, Guelph, Ontario.
1984   Maclean Hunter Building, College Park, Toronto.
1980   Mohawk College, Health Sciences Centre, Hamilton, Ontario.
1977   Palais de Justice, Kitchener, Ontario.
1975   University of Waterloo, Waterloo, Ontario.

Illustration de livres - Illustrated Books

Virgile. *Eclogues*, traduit par C. D. Lewis avec 23 lino-gravures (deux couleurs de Walter Bachinski) / translated by C. D. Lewis, with 23 two colour linocuts by Walter Bachinski. Publié par / Published by Shanty Bay Press, 1999.

Distinctions, prix et bourses - Honours, Awards, and Grants

1982   Bourse, Conseil des arts (court terme) pour études en France / Canada Council Short-Term Grant to study in France.
1978,79 Bourse, Conseil des arts (matériel) / Canada Council Materials Grant.
1978,79 Bourse, Conseil des arts de l'Ontario / Arts Council of Ontario Grant.
1974   Prix de l'Instituto Bancario S. Paolo di Tuono, (Prize), V Biennale (arts graphiques / graphic arts), Florence.
1973   Bourse, University of Guelph Research Advisory Board Grant.
Prix du mérite / Merit Prize, Los Angeles Printmaking Society, International Exhibition.
1971   Bourse, University of Guelph Research Advisory Board Grant.
Prix Albert Dumouchel, *Exposition internationale d'art graphique*, Montréal.
1969   Bourse, Conseil des arts (court terme) / Canada Council Short-Term Grant, pour la production

des lithographies *After Birth* par George C. Miller and Son, New York / for the production of portfolio of lithographs *After Birth*. Printed by George C. Miller and Son, New York.

Collections publiques - Public collections

Art Gallery of Brant, Brantford, Ontario
Art Gallery of Hamilton, Ontario
Art Gallery of Mississauga, Ontario
Art Gallery of North York, Ontario
Athabasca University, Alberta
Centre Saidye Bronfman, Montréal
Cad VISION, Calgary, Alberta
Cambridge Shopping Centres Ltd., Toronto
Canada Council Art Bank, Ottawa
Canadian Pacific Railways
Cineplex Odeon, Toronto
Museo Civico di bell art, Lugano, Suisse
Claridge Collection, Montréal
Drabinsky Collection, Toronto
Erindale College, University of Toronto
Esso Resources, Calgary
Gallery Stratford, Stratford, Ontario
General Foods of Canada, Toronto
Georgian College, Barrie, Ontario
Government of Ontario
Guaranty Trust, Toronto
Hammerson Canada, Toronto
Kitchener-Waterloo Art Gallery, Ontario
A.E. Lepage, Toronto
Los Angeles Printmaking Society, Los Angeles
McMaster University, Hamilton, Ontario
Ministère des Affaires étrangères, Canada
Mount St. Vincent University, Halifax, Nouvelle-Écosse
Musée des beaux-arts de Montréal, Montréal
Norcen Energy, Calgary, Alberta
OMERS, Toronto
Robert McLaughlin Art Centre, Oshawa, Ontario
Rothmans of Canada Collection, Toronto
Rodman Hall Art Centre, St. Catherines, Ontario
Royal Bank of Canada
Shell Canada Collection
Sun Life Insurance of Canada
The Tom Thomson Memorial Art Gallery, Owen Sound, Ontario
The Toronto Stock Exchange
University of Guelph
University of Iowa
University of Lethbridge
University of Manitoba
University of Windsor
Uffizi Gallery, Florence
Vancouver Art Gallery
Wilfred Laurier University, Waterloo, Ontario

I have been fortunate to have had continued support for my art for many years now. To Helen and Jacques Bellefeuille, my sincerest gratitude for this exhibition and the accompanying publication. Your dedication to the cause of contemporary art in Canada is passionate and unrivaled and I truly appreciate your continued support. I would also like to thank Crispin Elsted for his incisive and sensitive writing in this catalogue. I could not imagine a more wonderful introduction! He has put into words the relationship which I have only sensed between music, poetry and my work; he has captured the essence of what I do. And finally, my gratitude to Janis who shares with me a pastoral existence in Shanty Bay, and provided the inspiration for many of these works.

Walter, 2000

J'ai eu la chance de bénéficier d'un encouragement constant dans ma démarche artistique, et ce, depuis de nombreuses années. J'exprime ma sincère gratitude à Helen et à Jacques Bellefeuille pour la réalisation de cette exposition et du catalogue qui l'accompagne. Votre dévouement passionné à la cause de l'art contemporain au Canada est incomparable. Sachez que j'apprécie vraiment votre appui. Je voudrais également remercier Crispin Elsted pour son texte d'un ton incisif certes, mais qui témoigne d'une grande sensibilité. Je n'aurais pu imaginer une meilleur introduction. Il a su exprimer le rapport que j'avais pressenti entre la musique, la poésie et mon travail; il a parfaitement saisi l'essence de mon travail. Enfin, toute ma reconnaissance envers Janis qui partage avec moi une existence pastorale à Shanty Bay, et qui fourni l'inspiration à plusieurs de mes oeuvres.

Walter, 2000

Dépôt légal - Bibliothèque nationale du Québec, 2000
Dépôt légal - Bibliothèque nationale du Canada, 2000

ISBN 2-922173-08-9

Éditeur - Editor : GALERIE DE BELLEFEUILLE

Conception et réalisation
Concept and design : Andrés Duran
Collaboration : Anthony Collins, Martin Labrie
Photographie - Photography : Sarah Bachinski, John Bourosik,
David Milne
Textes - Contributors : Christian Elsted
Traduction - Translation : Christine Gendreau
Publié par - Published by : Galerie de Bellefeuille
Impression - Printer : Litho Acmé

Imprimé au Canada - Printed in Canada